For Brooklyn

Mommy and Daddy are so proud of you for reading 200,000 words last school year!

Table of Contents

1. Best Ball in the World
2. Popcorn and Pranks
3. Gone Without a Bounce
4. The Suspect List
5. The Rhino Riddle
6. Elephant-Sized Clues
7. Nighttime Zoo Mission
8. The Truth Bounces Out
9. Apologies and Antics
10. Party Under the Moon

📔 Booster's Journal: Entry #1

Bonus Material

Chapter One
Best Ball in the World

Booster was a big, fuzzy polar bear with an even bigger love for one thing—his big red ball.

It bounced.
It rolled.
It squeaked when he stepped on it just right.
To Booster, it wasn't just a ball. It was his best toy, his favorite friend, and his ultimate belly-flop target.

"Boing!" The ball bounced off a rock and soared through the air.

"Look out!" Lily called, ducking as the ball flew past her head.

Booster dove and slid across the grass, catching the ball with his paws and tumbling into a barrel of hay. *Pfff-thunk!*

"I meant to do that," he said, a little dazed, holding up the ball proudly.

Lily, a smaller polar bear with a lot more sass, rolled her eyes. "You and that ball. One day it's going to roll away and never come back."

Booster gasped. "Don't say that. She has feelings."

"She?"

Booster held the ball close. "Her name is Bouncette."

Lily stared at him. "You named your ball."

Booster shrugged. "You named your shadow that one time."

"Yeah, and *Shadowina* betrayed me," Lily said, narrowing her eyes. "She disappeared at noon."

Booster giggled. Then he stood up and gave the ball a mighty toss into the air. It bounced once, twice, and rolled behind the trees near the back of their enclosure.

Booster trotted after it. "Come on, Bouncette! Time for our lunchtime bounce-a-thon!"

But when he got to the spot…
The ball was gone.

Chapter Two

Popcorn and Pranks

Booster waddled out of the trees, scanning the grass. No red ball in sight.

"Lily," he called, "did you see where Bouncette went?"

Lily was lounging on a rock, licking honey off her paw like it was the most important thing in the world.

"Hmm?" she said without looking up. "Oh, the ball? Maybe it rolled into another dimension."

Booster blinked. "Another dimension?!"

Lily shrugged. "Could happen. Weird stuff happens around here."

Before Booster could panic any further, the smell of buttery popcorn floated through the air. His nose twitched. Lily perked up.

"Snack time!" they shouted together.

They followed their noses to the snack cart parked near the fence. Gordon, their friendly zookeeper with a big beard and a green uniform, was scooping popcorn into paper cones.

Gracie, his daughter, sat on the bench nearby with her feet swinging and a stuffed lion in her lap.

"Hey, bears!" Gordon called. "Hope you're hungry. Popcorn just popped."

Booster licked his lips. "Yes, please!"

Lily smirked. "Double scoop."

As Gordon handed out the snacks, Lily leaned in and whispered, "Watch this."

Before Booster could ask, she *stuffed* a pawful of popcorn into the back of his fluffy neck.

"AHHH! It's raining snacks!" Booster shouted, spinning in circles as popcorn flew everywhere.

Gracie burst out laughing. Even Gordon chuckled. "You two are a handful," he said, shaking his head.

Booster glared at Lily, puffing out his fur. "Very funny. I'll get you back, you know."

"Promises, promises," Lily said, tossing a kernel into her mouth.

Booster finished his snack and sighed. "Well… time to find Bouncette."

"You're still looking for that ball?" Lily asked, tilting her head.

Booster nodded. "Of course. She wouldn't just disappear."

Lily wiped her paws and stood up. "You're right. Balls don't disappear by themselves."

Then she smiled a little too big. Booster narrowed his eyes.

"Unless," Lily added, "someone *took* her."

Chapter Three
Gone Without a Bounce

Booster searched every corner of the enclosure. Behind the trees. Under the slide. Inside the old tire he sometimes napped in.

No red ball. No Bouncette.

"This doesn't make any sense," he muttered, crawling under a log. "She was *right here*."

A squirrel chattered at him from above, tossing an acorn that bounced off his nose.

"Hey!" Booster said, rubbing his snout. "Not helping!"

He flopped down on the grass and sighed. "She wouldn't just leave me…"

Across the yard, Lily was sipping from the water fountain like nothing was wrong.

Booster sat up straight. "LILY."

She looked over, cool as a snowflake. "What?"

"You're acting suspicious."

Lily raised one paw dramatically. "Suspicious? Me?"

"Yes, you! You were the last one near the ball. You made that weird joke about it disappearing. And now you're just... sipping."

"Is sipping a crime now?" she asked, batting her eyes.

Booster huffed. "If I find popcorn in Bouncette's spot, I'm calling it evidence."

Lily leaned casually against the fence, twirling a blade of grass in her paw.
"Maybe she didn't disappear," she said slowly. "Maybe someone *took* her."

Booster's eyes widened. "You think the *rhinos* took Bouncette?"

Lily shrugged. "They've got the muscle. And they've always looked a little... suspicious."

Booster turned dramatically and started marching toward the edge of the enclosure.

"I'm going to crack this case wide open."

Behind him, Lily grinned. "Hope you like mud."

Chapter Four
The Suspect List

Back in his cave, Booster dug through an old cardboard box until he found his most prized non-ball possession: his Detective Kit. It was really just a notebook, a pencil, and a pair of sunglasses he found behind the penguin exhibit. But it made him feel official.

He plopped down with a huff and opened the notebook to a fresh page.

At the top, he wrote in big, bold letters: **"SUSPECTS"**

Below that, he started a list:

1. **Lily** – *Definitely suspicious. Known prankster. Had popcorn. Smirked too much.*
2. **The Rhinos** – *Large. Strong. Quiet. Too quiet.*
3. **The Penguins** – *Always up to something. Distracting but sneaky.*
4. **Gordon** – *Has opposable thumbs. Access to tools.*
5. **Gracie** – *Small but smart. Might want ball for herself.*

He held the notebook up and squinted at it through the sunglasses. "This is bigger than I thought."

Lily peeked in from the cave entrance. "You done making your doodle diary?"

Booster flipped the notebook shut. "This is evidence. I'm building a case."

"Oh no, not another *Booster Investigation*," Lily said, flopping onto a nearby rock. "Last time you accused a turtle of stealing your scarf. Turned out you were wearing it."

"It was wrapped around my belly," Booster said defensively. "Camouflage!"

Lily chuckled. "So what's the plan, Detective Fuzz?"

"I start with the most obvious suspect," Booster said, sliding the sunglasses onto his nose. "I'm going to question the rhinos."

Lily raised an eyebrow. "And what if they charge?"

Booster gulped. "Then I'll charge back."

"You'll *cry* back."

"Details," he said, strutting out of the cave.

As Booster marched off toward the rhino yard, notebook in paw and sunglasses slightly crooked, Lily shook her head and grinned.

This was about to get interesting.

Chapter Five
The Rhino Riddle

Booster crept toward the rhino yard with all the stealth of a dancing walrus.

His paws squished through the mud. His notebook was tucked under one arm. His sunglasses had slid halfway down his nose. But he was focused.

"Detective Booster, on the case," he whispered to himself. "Time to sniff out the truth."

Two massive rhinos stood near the fence, snorting and munching on grass. One had a leaf stuck to her horn. The other was lying down, eyes half-closed like he was napping with his eyes open.

Booster cleared his throat. Loudly.

The leaf-horned rhino blinked. "Can we help you?"

"Yes," Booster said, standing tall. "I'm investigating a missing ball. Red. Round. Slightly squeaky. Have you seen it?"

The lying-down rhino grunted. "What's a bear doing in the mud zone?"

"Detective bear," Booster corrected, flipping open his notebook. "You two are on my suspect list."

"Why?" the leaf-horned rhino asked, clearly amused.

Booster pointed with his pencil. "You're strong. You're quiet. And Lily said you look suspicious."

The rhinos exchanged a look.

"Is Lily the small bear with the attitude?" asked the napping one.

"Yup."

"She says *everyone* looks suspicious."

Booster nodded slowly. "That's... actually fair."

The leaf-horned rhino chuckled. "Look, big guy. We haven't seen your ball. We mostly just nap, snack, and sit in mud."

Booster looked around. Mud everywhere. No sign of red.

"Hmm," he said, scribbling in his notebook. "Rhinos: grumpy, but not guilty... yet."

Just then, something red caught his eye. Booster spun around. Was it?

Nope. Just a ketchup packet someone dropped near the concession stand.

Booster sighed. "Sorry to bother you," he said, turning to leave.

"Wait," said the napping rhino. "You check with Ellie?"

Booster paused. "Ellie the elephant?"

"Yeah. She's always up before the sun. Sees everything."

Booster's eyes lit up. "She might've seen what happened to Bouncette!"

As he turned to go, the rhinos called after him, "Good luck, Detective!"

He puffed out his chest and saluted. "Justice never sleeps!"

Then he immediately slipped in a puddle and landed flat on his back.

"Justice needs a towel," Lily called from across the yard, cracking up.

Chapter Six
Elephant-Sized Clues

Ellie the elephant was the oldest animal in the zoo. She had wrinkles, wisdom, and a low, slow voice that made everything she said sound important—even if it was just about oatmeal.

Booster found her near the pond, gently flapping her ears and sipping water through her trunk.

"Excuse me, Miss Ellie," he said, puffing out his chest. "Detective Booster, reporting for questioning."

Ellie raised one eyebrow. "Questioning, hmm? This isn't about that time you accused the flamingos of running a secret noodle stand, is it?"

Booster turned red. "No. That was a misunderstanding."

"Mmm-hmm."

He cleared his throat. "This is serious. My ball—Bouncette—has vanished."

"Vanished?"

"Poof. Gone. Last seen yesterday afternoon."

Ellie blinked slowly. "Did you check under your snack barrel?"

"Yes."

"Inside the tire tunnel?"

"Yes."

"Behind Lily's bad attitude?"

Booster snorted. "Twice."

Ellie gave a tiny smile. "Well then... I did see something."

Booster leaned in. "You did?!"

"I was up early this morning. Around dawn. I saw Lily sneaking across the yard toward the fountain."

Booster gasped. "With the ball?"

Ellie nodded. "I believe so. Hard to miss that red blur in her paws. She looked... determined."

"Determined is her sneaky face!" Booster said, scribbling in his notebook like his pencil was on fire.

"She was muttering something too," Ellie added. "Something about paint, rockets, and the moon."

Booster's eyes widened. "Moon? Rockets? This is bigger than I thought."

Ellie leaned down and met his eyes. "Sometimes, Booster, when someone takes something... it's not because they're mean. It's because they don't know how to ask."

Booster froze. "Wait... are you saying Lily—"

"I'm saying," Ellie said gently, "you should talk to her before you plan a sting operation involving pigeons again."

Booster closed his notebook slowly.

"Thanks, Ellie," he said, then paused. "For real this time."

Ellie smiled. "Go get your answers, Detective."

Booster took a deep breath and started walking toward the fountain.

This case wasn't over.
It was just getting warm.

Chapter Seven
Operation Moonball

That night, while the zoo got quiet and the stars began to twinkle, Booster put on his sunglasses and tiptoed out of the cave.

Yes, it was nighttime.
Yes, it was very dark.
And yes, sunglasses made absolutely no sense.
But they made him feel cool. And brave.

"Operation Moonball is a go," he whispered.

He snuck past the flamingos (who were all asleep standing on one leg), ducked under the snack cart, and paused at the fountain.

Booster crouched low in a bush. His tail stuck out, but he felt hidden.

And then—movement.

Lily stepped out from behind a tree, holding something round and red.

Booster's breath caught in his throat. *It was Bouncette.*

Lily was humming to herself. She had a paintbrush in one paw and a small jar of glitter in the other.

GLITTER? Booster almost sneezed just looking at it.

He waited, watching as Lily carefully dabbed silver paint onto the ball, turning it into a sparkly, silvery... moon?

Booster popped out of the bush. "Aha! I knew it!"

Lily jumped, nearly dropping the paintbrush. "Booster?!"

"What are you doing with Bouncette?" he asked, confused and hurt.

Lily looked down. "I... I took her. I'm sorry."

"You *took* her?" Booster stepped closer. "Lily, you didn't even ask!"

"I know," she said quietly. "I thought it would be okay because I was using her for something good. I'm throwing a surprise Super

Moon Party for Gracie, and I wanted to make the ball look like the moon. But... I should've asked first."

Booster crossed his arms. "You should've. Even if your plan was nice, it still wasn't right to take something that wasn't yours."

Lily nodded. "I messed up. I got so excited about the party, I didn't think about how you'd feel."

Booster stared at Bouncette, now sparkling like the moon, then looked back at Lily.

"Well," he said, "I *am* mad… but I still want to help with the party."

Lily's face lit up. "Really?"

Booster sighed. "Yeah. Bouncette loves a good party. But next time, *ask*. Or at least leave a note."

Lily smiled sheepishly. "Deal."

They sat together under the stars, adding the final sparkles and making plans for the next day.

Even Bouncette squeaked in approval.

Chapter Eight
The Truth Bounces Out

The next morning, Booster yawned as he rolled out of his cave, glitter still clinging to his fur.

He spotted Lily near the fence, staring at the now fully painted ball.

"Hey," she said quietly.

"Hey," Booster replied.

There was a small pause.

"I've been thinking about what I did," Lily said, fidgeting with her paws. "I know I said sorry, but I really mean it. I wouldn't like it if someone took something important to me."

Booster looked down at Bouncette, now transformed into a glittering moon-ball masterpiece.

"Yeah," he said slowly. "You hurt my feelings, Lily."

She nodded. "I get it."

"But," Booster added, "you also made something pretty amazing. And I can tell you put a lot of heart into it."

Lily smiled a little. "Thanks for still helping me finish it."

Booster gave a half-smile. "It's what bears do. But let's just agree: next time you want to borrow something—"

"I ask," Lily said, finishing the sentence. "Or leave a really good snack as a bribe."

Booster snorted. "Deal."

Just then, Gordon and Gracie walked by the enclosure. Gracie gasped when she saw the sparkly moon ball resting on the grass.

"DAD! LOOK AT THAT!" she shouted, eyes wide.

Booster and Lily peeked out from behind a bush.

Gracie bounced up and down. "Can we throw a Super Moon Party?! Please?!"

Gordon chuckled. "If we do, I think we need to invite two very creative polar bears."

Lily turned to Booster. "I think this is going to be the best party ever."

Booster grinned. "Bouncette agrees."

And with that, the ball gave a happy little squeak—like she'd been in on the plan all along.

Chapter Nine

Apologies and Antics

The zoo was buzzing with excitement.

Balloons were tied to fences. A banner made from an old bedsheet hung between two trees that read **SUPER MOON PARTY!** In crooked letters. There was even a snack table stacked with popcorn, watermelon slices, and peanut butter sandwiches (Gordon's idea, obviously).

Booster and Lily stood near the entrance, watching Gracie dance in circles around the moon-ball.

"She really likes it," Lily said.

Booster nodded. "Yeah. You nailed it. I mean, we nailed it."

Lily gave him a grateful smile. "Thanks again for not staying mad."

Booster shrugged. "Well… I *was* mad. But I'm glad we talked it out."

Lily chuckled. "Next time, I promise—no secret plans involving your stuff."

Booster raised an eyebrow. "Even if it involves glitter?"

Lily sighed dramatically. "Even glitter."

Just then, the monkeys swung by the party and started pelting the snack table with banana peels. Booster dove to shield the watermelon.

Lily grabbed a cone of popcorn and launched a handful in the air like confetti. "Party's on!" she yelled.

Gracie giggled. Gordon shook his head. "Every time," he muttered with a smile.

Bouncette sat in the middle of it all—silver, sparkly, and proud. She didn't bounce much during the party, but she didn't have to.

She was the moon tonight.

As the sun set and the first star blinked in the sky, Lily leaned over to Booster.

"You know what this calls for?"

Booster raised a brow. "What?"

"A Bouncette sequel."

Booster grinned. "As long as she doesn't get *kidnapped* again."

"Borrowed!" Lily said, laughing.

"Same thing!"

And with a playful nudge, the two bears rolled into the grass, laughing under the stars as the party lit up around them.

Chapter Ten

Party Under the Moon

The sky turned deep blue as lanterns flickered on around the zoo.

Animals gathered from every corner—penguins waddled in, the flamingos swayed like dancers, and even the rhinos showed up, each wearing glow-stick necklaces (Gracie's idea, obviously).

Booster and Lily sat side by side, watching it all happen.

Bouncette glowed under the string lights, her glittery silver paint catching the moonlight just right.

"She looks happy," Booster said.

"She's a star," Lily agreed. "Or… a moon, I guess."

Gracie ran over and threw her arms around both bears. "Best. Party. Ever!"

Booster chuckled. "We aim to please."

Gordon gave them both a thumbs-up. "Remind me to hire you two for my next birthday."

As music played and laughter echoed through the zoo, Booster leaned back and smiled.

This wasn't just a party.
It was a reminder: when you talk things out, forgive one another, and work together—

Even a stolen (okay, borrowed) ball can turn into something beautiful.

And under the light of their handmade moon, Booster and Lily knew one thing for sure.

Every adventure was better… when shared.

THE END...or is it?

Booster's Journal

Entry #1: The Case of the Missing Bouncette

Today was *wild.*

First, my best friend (a red rubber ball named Bouncette) vanished without a trace. I went full detective mode. Made a list. Wore sunglasses. Questioned rhinos.

Then I found out Lily took her. At first, I was mad.....*really* mad. But then I found out why. She was planning a surprise party for Gracie. She just wanted to do something kind... she just didn't go about it the right way.

I told her it's not okay to take something without asking, even if you think it's for a good reason. And you know what? She *got* it. She really did.

We made things right.

We finished painting Bouncette to look like the moon.

And we threw the best Super Moon Party this zoo has ever seen.

I learned something today: Sometimes friends mess up. But if you talk, listen, and forgive... you can bounce back stronger.

(Also, I still don't trust the penguins. Just saying.)

Booster Bear

About the Author

Dr. Bernard Rutherford is a very serious, very human author who is *definitely not* a polar bear wearing sunglasses and typing with his paws.

He holds many impressive degrees from places you've probably never heard of, like the Institute of Snack Sciences and the Academy of Advanced Rolling. He enjoys long walks through zoo enclosures, in-depth detective work, and quietly observing animal behavior while pretending not to be part of it.

Dr. Rutherford has a deep appreciation for mystery, mischief, friendship, and well-balanced snacks. His hobbies include sneaky note-taking, advanced belly flopping, and suspiciously detailed knowledge of zoo layouts.

Although some readers have claimed he looks suspiciously like a certain polar bear they've read about, Dr. Rutherford insists that any resemblance is purely accidental.

Please respect his privacy. Or at least bring popcorn.

Lily's Blog

Stuffed Bunnies, Hot Dogs, and Rodent Drama

Posted by: Lily, Future Zoo Director & Full-Time Genius

Gracie brought a new stuffed bunny to the zoo today. Its name is *Carrots*.

It's soft. It's squishy. It has a bow. Everyone says it's the cutest thing in the world and keeps making high-pitched squealing sounds when they see it. I am *totally fine with this*.

Did I try to borrow Carrots for a closer look? Yes. Did I maybe take it back to my enclosure for a "safety inspection"?

Also yes. But it had a loose thread and I was being responsible. I'm a leader. Leaders are allowed to investigate plush rabbits.

Then there was the hot dog incident. The snack bar rolled out a new menu, and Holly nearly lost her mind when she heard someone order one. She actually hid behind the recycling bin until Gordon explained that hot dogs are not made from *actual* dogs. (I wasn't convinced at first either. The name is suspicious.) But then I tasted one. And okay… they're delicious. Like, really delicious. Still weirdly named, though.

Things escalated with the squirrel this week. I've started calling him *Greg* because it feels right. Greg is small, smug, and chaos in fur. He's hidden acorns in Booster's blanket, replaced my clipboard with a piece of bark, and most recently drew a picture of me with enormous ears on the break room whiteboard. It was actually kind of accurate, which made it worse.

So I did what any mature future zoo director would do—I made a "WANTED" poster and taped it to the tree near his nest. The next morning? Pinecone. Right to the face. Greg doesn't miss.

Oh, and guess who decided he needed a blog now? Booster. He saw me writing this and immediately launched **"The Booster Bulletin."** It's mostly snack reviews, nap ratings, and something called a "Feelings Forecast," which is just him drawing clouds over cartoon versions of himself. In today's edition, he drew a doodle of me frowning with the caption: "Lily, always watching." Which is true. But still rude.

Anyway, I've got to go. Greg is rustling leaves again and I don't trust it. I'm working on a blueprint for a squirrel-proof snack container and I still need to label the trapdoor section. More updates soon.

– Lily 🐾

Bear, Zoologist. Visionary.

Next up in the Booster Tales series...

BoosterTales: The Map Mishap

Booster finds a mysterious map blowing through the zoo. It has arrows, symbols, and a big red "X."

To Booster, that can only mean one thing: **buried treasure.**

But as he and Lily follow the clues, they discover something even more surprising…

Treasure doesn't always mean gold. And sometimes, the thing you dig up means the most to someone else.

Coming soon! Get ready for adventure, confusion, and at least one misidentified goat.

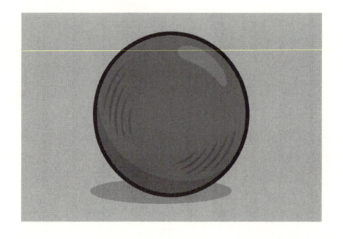

Oh yeah.... One more thing

Do YOU have a ball like Bouncette?!?

If yes: AMAZING.

If not: go find one IMMEDIATELY. This is urgent.

Because here's the deal **balls are the greatest thing ever invented.** (After snacks. And naps. And maybe popcorn. But it's CLOSE.)

There are a million (probably) games you can play with a ball. Here are a few I've tried. And by "tried," I mean "played until I fell over from joy."

Group Games:

4-Square – One square to rule them all. Bounce it, bop it, don't mess up like I always do in square 2.

9-Square in the Air – It's like volleyball if someone glued the rules to the sky. Absolute chaos. I LOVE IT.

Kickball – Like baseball, but with your feet! Warning: do not accidentally kick the ball into the snack cart. They get *weird* about that.

Soccer – Kick. Run. Trip. Repeat. SO MUCH RUNNING.

Solo Missions:

Bounce & Catch – Sounds easy. It's not. I have large paws.

Wall Ball – Bounce it off the wall and pretend you're a secret agent.

Balance Challenge – Try to balance it on your head while walking. (I made it 3 steps. Lily made it 40. It's fine.)

Name Your Ball – I named mine *Bouncette* and she's my best friend. 10/10 recommend.

Balls are more than toys.
They're sidekicks.
They're adventure starters.
They're round, bouncy bundles of possibility.

So go! Play! Bounce something! Fall over! Get back up!

(Then take a nap. You earned it.)

– Booster

Official Ball Enthusiast, Zoo League MVP, Professional Rolling Champion (self-declared)

Made in the USA
Columbia, SC
01 July 2025